SEYCHELLES TRAVEL GUIDE

The Ultimate Guide to Discovering the Best of Seychelles' Beaches, Culture, Islands, Food, and Activities. Everything You Need To Know Before Planning A Trip To Seychelles.

ANTHONY TURNER

Copyright © 2023 by Anthony Turner

All rights reserved. No part of this publication may be reproduced, distributed, or transmitted in any form or by any means, including photocopying, recording, or other electronic or mechanical methods, without the prior written permission of the publisher.

TABLE OF CONTENT

INTRODUCTION..5
    Why Visit Seychelles...7
    Brief History and Geography...10

CHAPTER 1:
PLANNING YOUR TRIP TO SEYCHELLES............12
    When to Go...13
    How to Get to Seychelles..15
    Getting Around Seychelles..17
    Where to Stay...19
    What to Pack..21
    Entry and Visa Requirements...23
    Currency and Language..25
    Suggested Budget...27
    Money Saving Tips...29
    Best Places to Book Your Trip..31

CHAPTER 2:
ISLAND HOPPING IN SEYCHELLES....................33
    Mahé Island...34

Praslin Island..37

La Digue Island.. 39

Other Islands to Visit..41

CHAPTER 3:
BEACHES AND WATER ACTIVITIES................... 43

Best Beaches in Seychelles.. 45

Snorkeling and Diving Spots..48

Surfing and Other Water Sports................................... 50

Boat Tours and Cruises... 52

CHAPTER 4:
WILDLIFE AND NATURE...................................... 54

Seychelles' Unique Flora and Fauna............................56

National Parks and Reserves..59

Birdwatching and Turtle Nesting................................. 61

Nature Walks and Hiking Trails................................... 63

CHAPTER 5:
FOOD AND DRINK IN SEYCHELLES................... 65

Seychellois Cuisine and Local Specialties..................... 67

Best Restaurants and Street Food................................69

Traditional Drinks and Cocktails..................................71

CHAPTER 6:

NIGHTLIFE AND ENTERTAINMENT IN SEYCHELLES..................73
    Nightclubs and Bars.. 75
    Casinos and Gaming...76
    Cultural Shows and Events..77
    Outdoor Movie Screenings...78

CHAPTER 7:
SHOPPING IN SEYCHELLES............................... 79
    Local Markets and Souvenirs.. 81
    Shopping Malls and Boutiques..................................... 83

CHAPTER 8:
CULTURE AND FESTIVALS................................ 85
    Art and Music Scene..87
    Festivals and Events Calendar......................................90
    Museums and Historical Sites...................................... 93

CHAPTER 9:
7-DAY ITINERARY IN SEYCHELLES.................... 96
    Day 1: Arrival Day..96
    Day 2: Beach Hopping and Water Activities..................97
    Day 3: Explore the Natural Wonders of Seychelles.......98
    Day 4: Explore Seychelles' Cultural Side..................... 100

Day 5: Cultural and Historical Tour............................ 101

Day 6: Island Hopping Adventure............................. 102

Day 7: Departure from Seychelles............................103

CHAPTER 10: PRACTICAL INFORMATION AND TIPS.. 105

Customs and Etiquette.. 105

Communication and Language.................................. 108

Simple Language Phrases to Know.............................110

Health and Safety Tips.. 112

Emergency Contacts..114

Communication and Internet Access..........................115

Useful Apps, Websites, and Maps...............................117

CONCLUSION.. 120

INTRODUCTION

Seychelles is a paradise on Earth, and I had the opportunity to visit this lovely country a few years ago. It was an unforgettable experience that I will never forget. I knew I was in for an adventure I'd never forget the moment I stepped off the plane.

The warm sun and cool sea wind greeted me as soon as I arrived. The beautiful beaches and blue ocean were breathtaking. I knew immediately that coming to Seychelles was the right decision.

I visited several islands during my stay, each one more beautiful than the last. I visited the well-known Anse Source d'Argent beach, famed for its clean waters, distinctive rock formations, and fine white sand. I also went to Praslin Island, where I saw the unique Coco de Mer palm, which is one of the world's rarest species.

Snorkeling was one of my favorite activities in Seychelles. The beautiful and colorful underwater world astounded me. The fish, corals, and other sea animals were breathtaking, and I felt as if I were swimming in an aquarium. I even got to swim with enormous sea turtles, which was a dream come true for me.

Seychelles is also known for its distinctive food, and I was eager to sample some of the local fare. Fresh shellfish and fish cooked in a typical Creole way were wonderful. I also tried several unusual fruits I'd never heard of, such as star fruit and jackfruit.

Finally, I must mention Seychelles people. They are some of the most welcoming, friendly, and warm people I have ever met. They made me feel at ease and guided me around the best of their nation.

I can still feel the warm sun on my skin, smell the salty sea air, and hear the waves smashing on the shore as I recall my time in Seychelles. It was an unforgettable experience I will remember for the rest of my life.

Why Visit Seychelles

Seychelles is a stunning archipelago of 115 islands in the Indian Ocean, off the coast of East Africa. This gorgeous country is recognized for its stunning beaches, blue waters, and lush foliage, making it a favorite tourist destination for visitors from all over the world. Here are some of the reasons why you should visit Seychelles.

Natural Beauty: Seychelles has some of the most gorgeous beaches in the world. Seychelles beaches are breathtaking, with crystal-clear waters, smooth white sand, and unusual rock formations. Popular beaches in Seychelles include Anse Source d'Argent, Beau Vallon, and Anse Intendance.

Wildlife: Seychelles is home to a number of unique and endangered creatures and birds, including giant tortoises, Seychelles warblers, and black parrots. While snorkeling or scuba diving in Seychelles, you can also see dolphins, whales, and several species of sea turtles.

Adventure: Adventure activities in Seychelles include snorkeling, scuba diving, kayaking, fishing, and surfing. You can also go climbing and trekking in Seychelles' beautiful rainforests, which are home to various unique plant and animal species.

Culture and History: Seychelles has a rich history and culture inspired by French, British, and African customs. You can learn about the country's colonial history and struggle for independence by visiting many museums and historical places.

Cuisine: The cuisine in Seychelles is distinct and diversified, influenced by French, Indian, and African influences. While admiring the gorgeous vistas of Seychelles, you can sample delicious seafood, exotic fruits, and traditional Creole meals.

Relaxation: Away from the hustle and bustle of daily life, Seychelles is an ideal spot to rest and relax. You can enjoy spa treatments, yoga, and meditation while admiring Seychelles' natural beauty.

In sum, Seychelles is a must-see destination for anyone who enjoys natural beauty, adventure, culture, and relaxation.

Seychelles offers a memorable experience that will last a lifetime, with its magnificent beaches, unusual fauna, and diversified food.

Brief History and Geography

Seychelles is a 115-island archipelago in the Indian Ocean northeast of Madagascar. The country has a population of roughly 100,000 people and an area of 459 square kilometers. The capital city of Seychelles is Victoria, which is located on the island of Mahé.

The Austronesians were the earliest immigrants in Seychelles, arriving around 2000 BC. Later, Arab and Persian traders visited the islands, followed by Portuguese explorers in the 16th century. In 1756, the French founded a colony in Seychelles and dominated the islands until 1810, when they surrendered to the British. Seychelles obtained independence from Britain in 1976 and became a Commonwealth nation.

Seychelles is a multicultural country having influences from Africa, Asia, and Europe. The official languages are English, French, and Creole, and the Roman Catholic faith is practiced by the majority of the population.

Seychelles' geography is dominated by its tropical environment and topography, which include granitic and coral islands surrounded by clear blue waters. Morne Seychellois, located on the island of Mahé, has the highest elevation in Seychelles at 905 meters. The islands also have various national parks and environmental reserves, including the UNESCO World Heritage Site Vallée de Mai National Park on Praslin Island.

Seychelles is a famous tourist destination noted for its stunning beaches, diversified culture, and distinctive fauna. The country has a flourishing tourism industry, which contributes significantly to its economy. Seychelles is a wonderful place to visit and discover because of its rich history, natural beauty, and multiculturalism.

CHAPTER 1:
PLANNING YOUR TRIP TO SEYCHELLES

Planning a trip to Seychelles can be an exciting and pleasurable experience, but it also demands meticulous planning to ensure a smooth and stress-free journey.

In this chapter, we'll go over the most important things to think about when arranging a vacation to Seychelles. We'll begin by talking about the optimum time to visit Seychelles and why it matters. Then we'll go over how to book your flights and accommodations, as well as how to get around Seychelles.

This chapter will provide you with the knowledge you need to organize a fantastic vacation to Seychelles, whether you're a first-time visitor or a seasoned traveler.

When to Go

When planning a trip to Seychelles, consider the timing of your visit. Seychelles has a tropical climate with temperatures ranging from 24°C to 32°C all year. However, there are two distinct seasons: the dry season and the wet season.

The dry season in Seychelles lasts from May to October and is considered the peak tourism season. During this time, you can expect lower humidity, fewer rain showers, and plenty of sunshine, making it an ideal time to visit the beaches and explore the islands. However, peak tourist season also means higher prices and more crowded beaches.

The wet season in Seychelles lasts from November to April and is marked by high humidity, periodic rain showers, and the threat of tropical storms. Despite the uncertain weather, the wet season might be an excellent time to visit Seychelles if you want lower pricing and less tourists.

Overall, the best time to visit Seychelles is determined by your travel choices and priorities. The dry season may be your best bet for beautiful skies and great beach conditions. However, if you're looking for lower prices and don't mind the occasional rain shower, the wet season can also be a great time to visit.

How to Get to Seychelles

The archipelago of Seychelles is situated in the Indian Ocean around 1,600 kilometers east of the continent of Africa. Due to its convenient international airport and a variety of transportation alternatives, Seychelles are not particularly difficult to reach despite their distant position. How to go to Seychelles is listed below:

By Air: Seychelles International Airport, which is situated on the main island of Mahé, serves as the country's main entry point. There are numerous reputable airlines that operate flights to Seychelles from significant cities all over the world, including Emirates, Etihad Airways, Qatar Airways, and Kenya Airways. Direct flights from a few cities are also provided by some carriers to Seychelles.

By Sea: You can travel to Seychelles by private yacht or by taking a cruise. There are numerous marinas and bays in Seychelles where you may moor your own yacht, and various cruise lines provide trips that include stops there.

Island-hopping: Using a domestic flight or ferry is a simple way to travel between islands once you've arrived in Seychelles. Regular ferry routes connect some of the islands, and a number of domestic airlines fly regularly between them.

Regardless of the route you use to get to Seychelles, it's important to plan your travel well in advance in order to guarantee availability and secure the best prices.

Getting Around Seychelles

Seychelles has effective and inexpensive transportation options, the country. Here are some of the ways of getting around Seychelles:

Domestic Flights: Several domestic airlines, including Air Seychelles and Zil Air, run frequent flights between Seychelles islands. These flights, which can be reserved online or through travel agencies, are an effective and practical way to get between islands.

Ferries: Some of Seychelles' islands may be reached by ferries. Between Mahé, Praslin, and La Digue, as well as other islands, Inter Island Ferry Seychelles offers frequent services. Compared to domestic flights, these ferries are more reasonably priced and can provide some breathtaking views of the nearby islands.

Taxis: Taxis are frequently available on Mahé's main island as well as Praslin and La Digue. Fares, especially for longer trips, can be high.

Car Rental: Another well known method of getting around Seychelles is by renting a car, particularly on the largest island, Mahé. In Seychelles, there are various domestic and international automobile rental firms that provide more economical solutions.

Public Bus: Mahé's major island has public buses that may be used to travel for a reasonable price. However, the bus schedules can occasionally be off, and the buses can become crowded during rush hours.

Overall, Seychelles' transportation options are practical and reasonably priced, enabling tourists to easily and independently explore the islands.

Where to Stay

Seychelles provides a variety of lodging choices to fit all preferences and financial ranges. You're sure to find something that meets your needs, whether you're looking for an opulent resort, a comfortable guesthouse, or a budget-friendly hostel. Some of the top places to stay in Seychelles are listed below:

Resorts: Seychelles are well-known for their opulent resorts, which provide everything from private villas with private pools to fine dining restaurants and top-notch spas. The Four Seasons Resort Seychelles, Constance Ephelia, and Hilton Seychelles Labriz Resort & Spa are a few of the most well-known resorts in Seychelles.

Guesthouses: Guesthouses are a more cost-effective choice and a wonderful opportunity to get a taste of the hospitality and culture of the area. Numerous inns provide cozy accommodations as well as amenities like swimming pools; some even include breakfast in their rates. Villa Vanilla, Buisson Guesthouse, and Le Domaine de La Reserve are a few of the top inns in Seychelles.

Self-Catering Accommodation: Seychelles offers self-catering options such flats and villas for people who value greater independence and privacy. These accommodations provide fully functional kitchens, enabling you to prepare your own meals and spend less money eating out.

Budget-Friendly Hostels: There are also hostels in Seychelles that provide economical housing for travelers on a tighter budget and backpackers. The Coco Blanche Backpackers, La Fontaine Holiday Apartments, and Vicky's Holiday Apartments are a few of the most well-liked hostels in Seychelles.

No matter where you choose to stay in Seychelles, you should reserve your lodging in advance to ensure availability and to obtain the best deals, especially during the busiest tourist times.

What to Pack

The climate, activities, and cultural customs of Seychelles should all be taken into account while preparing for a trip to Seychelles. For your trip to Seychelles, make sure to pack the following:

Lightweight and breathable clothing: Pack lightweight, breathable clothing made of natural fibers like cotton or linen because Seychelles have a tropical environment. For beach activities, hiking, and island exploration, bring comfortable clothing.

Swimwear: Seychelles is the ideal location for swimming and other water sports because to its stunning beaches and pristine waters. Pack your swimsuit or trunks.

Sun protection: The sun in Seychelles may be very strong, so it's vital to take sun protection gear like sunscreen with a high SPF, sunglasses, and a hat.

Insect repellent: Use insect repellant because Seychelles is a tropical place and because mosquitoes can be a problem, especially during the wet season. To avoid bites, carry bug repellent.

Comfortable walking shoes: Bring comfortable walking shoes because Seychelles is best experienced on foot, especially for hiking in the national parks.

Travel adapter: Bring a travel adaptor so you can charge your electronics because Seychelles utilizes British-style three-pin sockets.

Cash and credit cards: Although Seychelles is becoming increasingly card-friendly, it is still advised to have cash on hand for little purchases and for places that don't accept cards.

Respectful clothing: Modest dressing is required when attending places of worship because Seychelles is mostly a Catholic nation.

Keep in mind to pack lightly and make space in your luggage for any souvenirs and other goods you could pick up during your trip.

Entry and Visa Requirements

Depending on your nation of origin, there are different entry criteria for Seychelles. Here is a general overview of Seychelles' entry and visa requirements:

Visa-free nations: Citizens of a large number of nations, including those in the United States, Canada, and the European Union, are not required to obtain a visa in order to enter and remain in Seychelles for up to 90 days.

Visa on arrival: For a charge, visitors from a select group of nations, including those from China and India, can get a visa at Seychelles International Airport.

Advance visa application: Russia and Nigeria nationals, among others, are required to apply for a visa in advance of their journey to Seychelles.

Health requirements: Within 72 hours before departure, all travelers to Seychelles must have a negative COVID-19 PCR test result. Other health-related documents or vaccination records may also be required by some nations.

Passport requirements: All travelers to Seychelles must have a passport that is valid for at least six months after the date of entrance. Additionally, at least one blank page in your passport must be available for the entry stamp.

Before departing for Seychelles, it's crucial to confirm the precise entry and visa requirements for your country of origin. For additional information, get in touch with Seychelles embassy or consulate in your nation or check out the department's website.

Currency and Language

Seychelles rupee (SCR) is Seychelles' official currency. Seychelles rupee is available as coins worth 1, 5, and 10 rupees, as well as banknotes with denominations of 10, 25, 50, 100, and 500 rupees. In Seychelles, both US dollars and euros are often accepted, particularly at larger hotels and tourist destinations.

The three official languages of Seychelles are English, French, and Seychellois Creole. The official language of the government, business, and education is English, which is widely spoken.

Additionally widely spoken and taught in schools as a second language is French, particularly in the hospitality sector. Most Seychellois people speak Seychellois Creole, a creole language with a French foundation that is utilized in daily conversation.

It's advantageous to acquire a little bit of English and French before visiting Seychelles, especially if you intend to explore outside of the main tourist regions. For mingling with locals and really absorbing the culture, learning a few words of Seychellois Creole can be helpful. Several menus, signs, and other pieces of information can be found in English, French, and Seychellois Creole in Seychelles.

Suggested Budget

In comparison to many other locations in the region, Seychelles is generally regarded as a high-end destination with relatively expensive prices. There are, however, affordable ways to visit Seychelles. Here is a general overview of suggested spending limits for various categories of travelers:

Budget Travelers: The cost of living in Seychelles is often between $75 and $100 per day. This would include basic lodging in guesthouses or self-catering apartments, travel within the area, eating from the street, and activities like hiking and beachgoing.

Mid-Range Travelers: The typical daily budget for mid-range travelers visiting Seychelles is between $150 and $250 USD. This would include activities like island hopping and water sports, plush lodging in hotels or resorts, local transportation, dining at neighborhood eateries, and comfy accommodations.

Luxury Travelers: The typical daily budget for luxury travelers visiting Seychelles is between $500 and $1,000 or more. This would include opulent lodging at upscale resorts, upscale dining at restaurants, and upscale activities like spa treatments and excursions to private islands.

It's crucial to remember that rates in Seychelles might differ significantly based on the season, the type of lodging, and the activities. When setting a budget for their trip to Seychelles, visitors should also account for the cost of their flights and visas.

Money-Saving Tips

Although Seychelles is regarded as a luxury destination, there are still ways to cut costs on your trip there. Here are some suggestions for how to save money:

Travel During the Off-Season: Seychelles' busiest travel period, from December to April, is also the most expensive. Think about going between May and November when travel costs are typically lower.

Choose Budget-Friendly Accommodation: Seychelles offers a wide range of affordable lodging options, including hostels, self-catering apartments, and guesthouses. These solutions can save you a ton of money because they are sometimes far less expensive than hotels and resorts.

Cook Your Meals: If you're staying in self-catering accommodation, you might want to cook your meals because eating out can be pricey in Seychelles. You might significantly reduce your meal costs by doing this.

Use Public Transportation: Taxis can be pricey in Seychelles; instead, think about taking the bus or, if you feel comfortable driving on the left side of the road, renting a car.

Book Activities in Advance: Online reservations can often be made for a lesser price than on-site reservations for many popular Seychelles activities, such as boat cruises and water sports.

Stick to Free Activities: Seychelles is renowned for its stunning beaches, hiking trails, and natural parks, many of which are open to the public free of charge. To save money on your trip, stick to activities that are free.

You can take advantage of Seychelles' natural beauty without going over budget by using these money-saving tips.

Best Places to Book Your Trip

Travel to Seychelles can be booked through a variety of websites and travel companies. Some of the top locations for Seychelles travel bookings are listed below:

Expedia: Expedia is a well-known online travel agency that provides travel packages, hotels, and flights to Seychelles. They frequently have offers and discounts.

TripAdvisor: TripAdvisor is an excellent resource for finding reviews and suggestions for Seychelles lodging and activities. They also facilitate hotel and holiday rental reservations.

Booking.com: This well-known website for making reservations has a variety of lodging options in Seychelles, ranging from affordable guesthouses to opulent resorts.

Vacation homes in Seychelles can be found on the well-liked website Airbnb, which is a perfect choice for tourists on a tight budget.

Travel Agencies: Numerous travel agencies focus on Seychelles vacations. These organizations frequently provide tailored itineraries and bundle bargains that might help you save money.

It's crucial to conduct thorough research before making travel arrangements to Seychelles and to check costs and customer ratings on several booking sites to make sure you're getting the best bargain.

CHAPTER 2:
ISLAND HOPPING IN SEYCHELLES

Anyone visiting the archipelago of Seychelles should go island hopping. Island hopping provides an opportunity to see the diversity of Seychelles' 115 islands and their natural beauty, culture, and history. Each island has its distinct appeal.

Everything you need to know about island hopping in Seychelles will be covered in this chapter, including the best islands to visit, and advice on how to get the most out of your island-hopping experience.

Island hopping in Seychelles offers limitless opportunities for adventure and leisure, whether you're hoping to unwind on gorgeous beaches, stroll through lush forests, or learn about the local cuisine and culture. Come along with me as we go island hopping to discover the best of Seychelles.

Mahé Island

The largest and most populous island in Seychelles is Mahé Island, which is renowned for its breathtaking beaches, lush tropical woods, and vibrant indigenous culture. Mahé, which has a population of about 80,000, is home to numerous other thriving cities and villages, including the capital city of Victoria.

The stunning beaches on Mahé Island are one of its key draws. The island's most well-known beaches, each of which offers a distinctive experience, include Beau Vallon Beach, Anse Intendance, and Anse Royale. The busiest beach on Mahé is Beau Vallon Beach, which offers a wide variety of water sports and beach activities. Anse Intendance, on the other hand, is a more remote and tranquil choice for those seeking to avoid crowds.

Mahé Island is home to many parks and environmental reserves in addition to its beaches, notably the Morne Seychellois National Park. This park, which makes up over 20% of the island, is home to numerous rare and indigenous plant and animal species as well as several hiking trails for the more daring tourists.

Mahé Island has several museums and historical sites to tour for individuals who are curious about the local way of life. The Victoria Clocktower and the Sir Selwyn Selwyn-Clarke Market offer a look into the island's colonial past, while Seychelles National Botanical Gardens and Seychelles Natural History Museum are well-liked destinations for learning about the island's flora and animals.

Mahé Island boasts a thriving restaurant and bar scene with a variety of local and international cuisine available for eating and nightlife. The island is known for its fresh seafood, and several eateries offer dishes made with just-caught fish.

Mahé Island offers a variety of lodging alternatives, from luxurious resorts to inexpensive guesthouses, many of which are located in or close to the island's well-known beach areas. Regular flights from important international airports to Seychelles International Airport make the island accessible as well.

Overall, Mahé Island provides visitors with a wide variety of experiences, from unwinding on its gorgeous beaches to discovering its verdant forests and rich culture. Anyone visiting Seychelles should make sure to stop there.

Praslin Island

The second-largest island in Seychelles, Praslin Island, is renowned for its breathtaking beaches, clean waters, and distinctive flora and wildlife. The island is easily reachable by ferry or airplane and is situated around 44 kilometers northeast of Mahé Island.

The Vallée de Mai Nature Reserve, a UNESCO World Heritage Site that is home to the rare and indigenous Coco de Mer palm tree, is one of the main draws on Praslin Island. The reserve is also home to several other rare plant and animal species, including the black parrot, one of the world's most endangered bird species.

The Anse Lazio beach, which is routinely rated as one of the best beaches in the world, is another well-liked destination on Praslin Island. The beach is the ideal location for swimming, snorkeling, and sunbathing because of its beautiful white sand, clear blue waters, and lush green surroundings.

Praslin Island has a variety of water sports opportunities, including scuba diving, snorkeling, and fishing. Visitors can also take advantage of several boat cruises to explore the nearby islands and their lovely beaches.

Praslin Island is known for its natural beauty, but it also boasts a vibrant cultural heritage. The Praslin Museum, which sheds light on the island's colonial past, and St. Anne Chapel, which goes back to the early 1800s, are just two of the museums and historical sites that can be found on the island.

On Praslin Island, lodging options range from affordable guesthouses to opulent resorts, with a large number of choices available in or close to the popular beach areas. Regular flights from Mahé Island and other surrounding islands to Praslin Island Airport make the island accessible as well.

Overall, Praslin Island is a must-see location for visitors to Seychelles because it provides a rare combination of scenic natural beauty, cultural experiences, and chances for relaxation and adventure.

La Digue Island

A short ferry trip separates Praslin Island from La Digue Island, a tiny Seychelles island. It is well-known for its magnificent beaches, beautiful waters, and laid-back environment. From Mahé Island, you can use a ferry or a helicopter to go to the island.

The Anse Source d'Argent beach, regarded as one of the most stunning beaches in the world, is one of the main draws on La Digue Island. The beach is the ideal location for swimming and snorkeling because of its magnificent rock formations and crystal-clear waters. The island's natural reserve, which is home to a variety of native plants and animals, is also accessible to tourists.

The L'Union Estate, a former plantation that has been turned into a living museum, is another well-liked destination on La Digue Island. To learn about the island's traditional way of life, including copra cultivation, vanilla farming, and boat building, visitors can take a tour of the estate.

La Digue Island has a variety of adventurous activities available, such as cycling and trekking. Visitors can rent bicycles to tour the island's quaint communities and stunning natural settings. Hiking routes take you to breathtaking vistas and remote beaches.

Small guesthouses and opulent resorts are both available on La Digue Island. Visitors have the option of lodging close to the beach or on the island's quaint village, which has a selection of boutiques, eateries, and pubs.

La Digue Island is a stunning and tranquil location that shouldn't be missed when traveling to Seychelles. It is the ideal destination for anyone looking for a serene and natural retreat due to its beautiful beaches, fascinating history, and laid-back environment.

Other Islands to Visit

Other lesser-known islands in Seychelles, besides Mahé, Praslin, and La Digue, are worthwhile trips. Several of these islands are:

Silhouette Island: This island, which is close to Mahé Island, is renowned for its luxuriant jungles, unusual fauna, and stunning beaches. In the pristine waters, visitors can go hiking, birdwatching, or snorkeling.

Cousine Island is a little private island next to Praslin Island that is well-known for its gorgeous beaches and opulent lodgings. To discover the island's distinctive flora and fauna, visitors can go snorkeling, kayaking, or on a guided nature walk.

Bird Island is a sanctuary for birdwatchers, as its name suggests. Bird Island, which is close to Mahé Island, is home to numerous bird species, including the endangered Seychelles magpie robin. Additionally, visitors can go fishing, snorkeling, or on a nature walk to discover the island's natural beauty.

Curieuse Island is known for its enormous tortoises, which may be seen freely roaming the island. Curieuse Island, which is close to Praslin Island, boasts stunning beaches as well as trekking paths.

Félicité Island is a tiny island next to La Digue Island that is well-known for its exclusive resorts and isolated beaches. In the crystal-clear seas, visitors can enjoy kayaking or snorkeling, or just unwinding on the gorgeous beaches.

When visiting Seychelles, one must not pass up the opportunity to experience these islands specially and unforgettably. The distinct characteristics and attractions of each island make them ideal for anyone seeking an exciting and varied island-hopping trip.

CHAPTER 3:
BEACHES AND WATER ACTIVITIES

Seychelles is well known for its stunning beaches and pristine waters, making it the perfect place for people seeking a peaceful beach vacation. Some of the most beautiful beaches in the world may be found throughout the archipelago, each with its special attributes and attractions. Seychelles offers a variety of water sports, such as kayaking, fishing, and snorkeling, in addition to beach relaxation.

The top beaches and water activities in Seychelles will be covered in this chapter. On each of the major islands, including Mahé, Praslin, and La Digue, we'll focus on the best beaches.

We will go over the finest locations for snorkeling and diving as well as where to rent equipment for those interested in water sports. We'll also look into the other water sports accessible, such as windsurfing, stand-up paddling, and kayaking.

Seychelles has activities for everyone, whether you choose to spend your day quietly unwinding on the beach or partaking in some thrilling water sports. Grab some sunscreen and let's get started!

Best Beaches in Seychelles

Seychelles are well known for its breathtaking beaches with beautiful, blue waters, fine sand, and verdant surroundings. The islands are home to more than 100 stunning beaches, each of which is distinctive in its way. Some of the top beaches in Seychelles are listed below:

Anse Source d'Argent, La Digue Island - With its distinctive granite rocks and emerald-colored seas, this beach is possibly the most photographed in the world. Additionally, it's one of Seychelles' busiest beaches.

Anse Lazio, Praslin Island - This beautiful beach is well-known for its granite rocks, crystal-clear waves, and fine white sand. One of the best beaches in the world, according to rankings, is this one.

Beau Vallon, Mahé Island One of the most well known beaches in Seychelles is Beau Vallon on Mahé Island. It is renowned for its expansive stretches of silky white sand, clean waters, and breathtaking sunsets.

Petite Anse, La Digue Island - La Digue Island's Petite Anse is a remote beach that can only be reached by boat or on foot through a dense jungle. It's the ideal location for a quiet swim or a romantic picnic.

Anse Georgette, Praslin Island - One of the most beautiful beaches in Seychelles is Anse Georgette on Praslin Island, which features blue waves, smooth white sand, and breathtaking surroundings. It is a little more isolated than other well-known beaches, making it ideal for people seeking a peaceful time.

Anse Intendance, Mahé Island - Anse Intendance on Mahé Island is a well-liked surfing location with waves that can grow to a height of ten feet. It's a fantastic location for swimming and tanning as well.

Anse Coco, La Digue Island - Anse Coco on La Digue Island is an isolated beach that can only be reached by hiking through a dense jungle. It's the ideal location for a tranquil swim and to take in Seychelles' breathtaking natural beauty.

These are only a few of Seychelles' numerous beautiful beaches. It's worthwhile exploring new beaches on different islands to find your personal favorites.

Snorkeling and Diving Spots

Due to its clean seas, rich marine life, and breathtaking coral reefs, Seychelles is a well-known snorkeling and diving destination. Some of the top diving and snorkeling locations in Seychelles are listed below:

Aldabra Atoll - Aldabra Atoll is a UNESCO World Heritage Site that is home to some of the most pristine coral reefs in the entire world as well as a variety of fish, including sharks, turtles, and manta rays.

Sainte Anne Marine National Park - Near Mahé Island's coast is Sainte Anne Marine National Park, which has some of the top diving and snorkeling locations in Seychelles. Diverse coral gardens, limestone formations, and underwater caverns are available for exploration by tourists.

Curieuse Island - Hawksbill turtles can be seen while snorkeling or scuba diving in the area around Curieuse Island, which is a small island with a robust population of them.

Denis Island - Due to its pristine waters and abundance of marine life, Denis Island is a well-liked diving location. Divers can explore a variety of dive spots, including a wall that drops 90 meters into the depths below.

Conception Island - Conception Island is a small island next to Praslin Island that is well-known for its coral reefs, fish, and other marine life. It is also a great place to go diving and snorkeling.

Shark Bank - Shark Bank is a well-liked location for snorkeling and scuba diving with friendly reef sharks, despite its frightening moniker. Rays and turtles are among the other marine animals that tourists might see.

Baie Ternay Marine Park - Octopuses, stingrays, and turtles are among the many marine animals that call Baie Ternay Marine Park, which is on Mahé Island's northwest coast, home.

These are only a few of Seychelles' many world-class snorkeling and diving locations. In Seychelles' crystal-clear seas, there is something to explore for everyone.

Surfing and Other Water Sports

Even though Seychelles isn't as well known for surfing as some other tropical locations, it still presents some fantastic opportunities for surfers and other water sports enthusiasts. The following are a few of the top water activities in Seychelles:

Surfing - Between May and September, when the waves are at their greatest, is the best time to go surfing in Seychelles. Anse Intendance on Mahé Island, where surfers may catch some exceptional reef breaks, is the most well-known surf location in Seychelles.

Windsurfing and kitesurfing - Seychelles are a fantastic location for windsurfers and kitesurfers thanks to the year-round consistency of the trade winds. Anse Lazio and Anse Georgette on Praslin Island, as well as Anse Royale and Beau Vallon on Mahé Island, are some of the top locations for windsurfing and kitesurfing.

Jet Skiing and Parasailing - Jet skiing and parasailing are also well-liked activities on the Islands for people who love motorized water sports. Jet ski rentals and guided tours are available for tourists to explore the shoreline, while parasailing provides a fascinating aerial view of the islands.

Snorkeling and Scuba Diving - Snorkeling and scuba diving are popular activities in Seychelles for people who want to explore the undersea environment, even if they aren't officially water sports. Due to the pristine waters and wealth of marine life, Seychelles provide some of the best snorkeling and diving in the world.

Stand-up Paddleboarding - Stand-up paddleboarding (SUP) is a great way to explore Seychelles' calm, shallow waters. Visitors may explore the coastline and find undiscovered coves and beaches by renting SUP boards or going on guided trips.

Seychelles offers a variety of activities to keep you occupied while on the trip, whether you're an experienced surfer or a novice water sports lover. There is no shortage of entertainment in Seychelles because of its pristine waters and stunning beaches.

Boat Tours and Cruises

Boat tours and cruises are very popular among Seychelles visitors. Here are a few suggestions for boat tours and cruises:

Island Hopping Tours - Seychelles has over 100 islands, and island hopping trips are a terrific way to see them all and learn about their unique characteristics. Some itineraries even include visits to isolated islands and quiet beaches.

Sunset Cruises - Sunset cruises are a popular way to watch the sunset over the Indian Ocean. Many tours include dinner or drinks on board, which makes for a romantic evening.

Fishing Charters - Seychelles is recognized for its outstanding fishing, and fishing charters are a popular activity for visitors. Visitors can expect to catch a variety of fish depending on the time of year, including tuna, marlin, and sailfish.

Glass Bottom Boat Tours - For those who prefer to stay dry, glass bottom boat trips are an excellent opportunity to experience Seychelles' underwater environment. These cruises provide views of vibrant coral reefs, tropical fish, and other sea life.

Luxury Yacht Charters - Visitors can opt for a luxury yacht charter for a truly luxurious experience. With bespoke itineraries and gourmet dining options, these charters provide a private and exclusive way to explore the islands.

Whatever type of boat tour or cruise you choose, you'll enjoy the breathtaking views of Seychelles' turquoise waters and picturesque islands.

CHAPTER 4:
WILDLIFE AND NATURE

Seychelles is a nature lover's paradise, with its various ecosystems and distinct flora and fauna. Visitors may explore the islands' national parks and reserves, go birdwatching and sea turtle hatching, and enjoy nature walks and hiking routes through some of the world's most pure and unspoiled natural surroundings.

Seychelles is home to several endemic plant and animal species, many of which are unique to the island. On Praslin Island, visitors can explore the Vallée de Mai Nature Reserve, a UNESCO World Heritage site that is home to the legendary coco de mer palm as well as a variety of bird and animal species. The Aldabra Atoll, one of the world's largest coral atolls and a UNESCO World Heritage site is also home to a rich range of flora and animals, including giant tortoises, unusual birds, and marine life.

The many bird species present on the islands, including the Seychelles warbler, Seychelles magpie-robin, and Seychelles blue pigeon, will excite birdwatchers. The islands are also a popular nesting place for green and hawksbill turtles, with tourists able to see the turtle eggs hatch and hatchlings emerge on select beaches.

Nature walks and hiking trails are a terrific opportunity to enjoy the natural beauty of Seychelles, with numerous national parks and reserves offering guided walks and hikes. Visitors can take a stroll through Mahé Island's Morne Seychellois National Park or face the more difficult paths of Praslin Island's Fond Ferdinand Nature Reserve.

Seychelles has plenty to offer, whether you're a nature enthusiast or simply looking for a calm and refreshing experience in a gorgeous natural location. The islands are a nature lover's dream come true, with their unique flora and fauna, national parks, and environmental reserves.

Seychelles' Unique Flora and Fauna

Seychelles is home to a wide variety of flora and fauna, many of which are native to the islands. Because of the Islands' seclusion and unusual geology, several species that are found nowhere else on the planet have evolved.

The coco de mer palm, which produces the world's largest seed and is exclusively found on Praslin and Curieuse Islands, is one of Seychelles' most prominent plant species. The jellyfish tree, the Seychelles pitcher plant, and the Seychelles paradise flycatcher are also peculiar to Seychelles.

The wildlife of the Seychelles is likewise unusual, with a variety of endemic bird and mammal species. Among the various bird species found on the islands are the Seychelles warbler, Seychelles magpie-robin, and Seychelles blue pigeon. The Aldabra giant tortoise, one of the world's largest tortoise species, can only be found in the Aldabra Atoll.

The marine life surrounding Seychelles is similarly rich and distinctive. A variety of indigenous fish species live on the islands, including the Seychelles clownfish and the Seychelles damselfish. While snorkeling or diving, visitors can see whale sharks, manta rays, and other marine life.

Seychelles takes great pride in its efforts to maintain its unique flora and fauna, having established various national parks and nature reserves to protect these species and their ecosystems. Visitors to the islands can learn about these conservation initiatives and see firsthand the splendor of Seychelles' unique flora and fauna.

National Parks and Reserves

Several national parks and nature reserves protect the islands' unique biodiversity in Seychelles. Here are a few of the most notable:

Vallée de Mai Nature Reserve: This nature reserve on Praslin Island is home to the iconic coco de mer palm, as well as numerous endemic plant and bird species.

Morne Seychellois National Park: This national park, which covers more than 20% of Mahé Island's total land area, offers hiking paths and breathtaking views of the island's mountains and woods.

Aldabra Atoll: A UNESCO World Heritage Site, Aldabra Atoll is home to the world's biggest elevated coral atoll and the Aldabra giant tortoise, among other unusual species.

Curieuse Marine National Park: This marine national park, located off the coast of Praslin, is recognized for its beautiful coral reefs and sea turtle nesting places.

Aride Island Nature Reserve: This little island north of Praslin is home to many uncommon bird species, including the Seychelles warbler and the Seychelles magpie-robin.

Visitors to these national parks and nature reserves can take guided tours, go on nature walks, and go on birdwatching expeditions, as well as learn about the conservation efforts being made to maintain these unique ecosystems.

Birdwatching and Turtle Nesting

Seychelles is home to a wide range of bird species, many of which are endemic and found nowhere else on the planet. Some of the best sites to go birding are:

Cousin Island: A birdwatcher's dream, this small granitic island is home to various species of seabirds, including the Seychelles warbler, Seychelles magpie-robin, and the uncommon Seychelles sunbird.

Bird Island: As the name implies, Bird Island is a birdwatcher's paradise, especially during the breeding season, which runs from May to September, and sees tens of thousands of sooty terns and other seabirds nest on the island.

Aride Island: This little granitic island is home to a variety of bird species, including the endangered Seychelles white-eye, Seychelles warbler, and Seychelles magpie-robin.

In addition to birding, Seychelles is a popular turtle nesting site. Hawksbill and green turtles have been observed nesting on several of the islands, notably Mahé's Anse Intendance and La Digue's Grand Anse. Visitors can see these gentle giants nesting and hatching while learning about conservation efforts to save these endangered species.

Nature Walks and Hiking Trails

Natural beauty abounds in Seychelles, and one of the best ways to appreciate it is through nature hikes and hiking paths. Various hiking paths allow visitors to discover the natural beauty of the islands, ranging from lush rainforests to magnificent coastline vistas.

The following are some of the most popular nature walks and hiking routes in Seychelles:

Morne Seychellois National Park: This Mahé Island national park has a variety of hiking paths ranging from short nature walks to strenuous hikes. Visitors can explore the park's lush jungles, look for endemic bird species, and take in the breathtaking vistas of the surrounding mountains and coastline.

Vallee de Mai Nature Reserve: This UNESCO World Heritage site on Praslin Island is home to the famed Coco de Mer palm tree, which produces the world's largest seed. Visitors can enjoy a stroll through the forest, viewing rare bird species, and learning about Seychelles' distinctive flora and fauna.

Anse Major: Hikers can enjoy stunning views of the Indian Ocean from this gorgeous coastline trail on Mahé Island, which winds through lush flora and rocky terrain. The walk concludes with Anse Major Beach, which is quiet and ideal for swimming.

Copolia Trail: Hike up to the summit of Copolia mountain on Mahé Island for panoramic views of the island and the Indian Ocean. The trail is steep and difficult, but the vistas are well worth it.

Seychelles has something for everyone, whether you want to take a peaceful nature walk or a strenuous excursion. Remember to bring your camera to capture the breathtaking sights along the journey!

CHAPTER 5:
FOOD AND DRINK IN SEYCHELLES

When planning your trip to Seychelles, don't forget to check out the country's diverse and unique food scene. Seychellois cuisine is a fusion of African, French, Indian, and Chinese influences, resulting in a wide range of delectable dishes sure to please any palate.

This chapter will go deeper into Seychellois cuisine and local delicacies, such as grilled fish with Creole sauce, octopus curry, and coconut fish curry. You'll discover the spices and tastes that give Seychellois food its particular character.

But it's not just the food that makes Seychelles unique. The dining experience is unrivaled. Seychelles has something for everyone, from sophisticated dining to street food. We'll visit the top restaurants in Seychelles, from those with magnificent ocean views to those hidden away in the hills, serving up some of the country's most exquisite dishes. We'll also show you the best street food options, where you can eat Seychellois snacks and local cuisine at low costs.

In Seychelles, no dinner is complete without a drink to wash it down. We'll introduce you to traditional Seychelles drinks and cocktails, such as Takamaka Rum, fresh coconut water, and the delightful Coco D'amour. We'll also show you the best spots to drink, from coastal pubs to trendy lounges.

In this chapter, you will find everything you need to know about Seychelles' food and drink scene, whether you're a foodie or just looking to experience some new flavors. So get ready to excite your taste buds and enjoy Seychelles' culinary treasures!

Seychellois Cuisine and Local Specialties

The cuisine of the Seychelles is a fusion of African, French, Chinese, and Indian influences, resulting in a distinct and tasty culinary experience. With so much fresh fish, tropical fruits, and veggies available, it's no surprise that Seychelles has evolved a cuisine that emphasizes these indigenous components.

The popular Seychellois curry, which is often made with fish, octopus, or chicken and served with rice or breadfruit, is one of the local specialties that visitors should not miss. Grilled fish, which is often seasoned with local spices and served with chutney or salad, is another favorite dish. Tec-tec, a type of shellfish served in a rich tomato sauce, and shark chutney, a spicy delicacy prepared from shark meat, are two other must-try delicacies.

Local snacks and street cuisine, such as samosas, bouchons (deep-fried sweet potato balls), and coconut bread, are also available to visitors. There are lots of sweet options, such as ladob, a dessert comprised of bananas, sweet potatoes, and coconut milk, and fruit salads with tropical fruits including mango, papaya, and pineapple.

Overall, the cuisine of Seychelles is diversified and tasty, reflecting the island nation's rich cultural past and natural riches.

Best Restaurants and Street Food

Seychelles is a foodie's delight, with cuisine blending Creole, French, Indian, Chinese, and African influences. There are numerous possibilities for satisfying your taste senses, ranging from fine dining restaurants to street food vendors. The island nation is well-known for its fresh seafood, tropical fruits, and delicious spices, all of which are employed in a variety of meals.

The capital city of Victoria on Mahé Island, where you can find a range of restaurants serving traditional delicacies such as fish curry, octopus salad, and coconut milk-based dishes, is one of the greatest sites to enjoy Seychellois cuisine. Check out the local street food scene for grilled fish, fresh fruit, and savory snacks like samosas and coconut fritters for a more relaxed eating experience.

Seychelles boasts several award-winning restaurants that exhibit the country's food in a more contemporary style for those searching for a high-end culinary experience. These restaurants frequently integrate international flavors and current techniques into their cuisine, resulting in a distinct flavor fusion.

No matter where you eat, sample some of the local specialties like shark chutney, fruit bat curry, and Ladob, a dessert made with banana, coconut milk, and vanilla. Don't forget to wash it all down with a refreshing local beer or a fruity drink crafted with fresh tropical ingredients.

Traditional Drinks and Cocktails

When it comes to drinks and cocktails in Seychelles, there are numerous traditional alternatives. Palm wine, commonly known as "kalou," is a popular drink prepared from the sap of the coconut palm tree. This drink has a sweet and somewhat sour flavor and is popular among the locals.

Another popular beverage is "bacca," a form of handmade rum laced with herbs and spices such as cinnamon and cloves. This beverage is frequently consumed at special occasions and celebrations.

Non-alcoholic options include "santol," a delightful drink prepared from the juice of the santol fruit blended with sugar and water. "Alouda" is another popular non-alcoholic beverage made with milk, basil seeds, and flavored syrup.

The "seychellois martini" is a must-try when it comes to cocktails. This cocktail combines Takamaka rum, a local favorite, with passionfruit juice, lime juice, and honey. The "seabreeze," a blend of vodka, grapefruit juice, and cranberry juice, is another popular cocktail.

Many bars and restaurants in Seychelles serve international drinks and cocktails, but it's worth trying the local options to get a true taste of the island's culture.

CHAPTER 6: NIGHTLIFE AND ENTERTAINMENT IN SEYCHELLES

Welcome to the wonderful world of Seychelles' nightlife and entertainment! This gorgeous island nation offers a variety of entertaining and vivid entertainment alternatives that will keep you engaged long into the night, from nightclubs and bars to beach parties, casinos, and live music performances.

Seychelles has a plethora of nightclubs and pubs to pick from if you're searching for a busy night out. You'll find something to fit your tastes, whether you're looking for a sophisticated and contemporary rooftop bar or a more laid-back beachside spot.

Seychelles' beach parties are a must-see for people who want to dance under the stars. What better way to enjoy the island vibes than with a martini in hand and dancing to the beat of the music?

Why not try your luck at one of Seychelles' casinos if you're feeling lucky? You never know when you might score the jackpot with so many different games and slot machines.

Seychelles, in addition to the normal nightlife alternatives, offers cultural presentations and events like traditional dance performances, music concerts, and outdoor cinema screenings. You can even take a sunset sail with your loved ones, admiring the view while enjoying a cool beverage.

Whatever your preferences are, Seychelles' nightlife and entertainment scene has something for everyone. So, prepare to let your hair down and enjoy the vibrant energy of this stunning island nation!

Nightclubs and Bars

Seychelles is famous for its natural beauty, but it also offers a vibrant nightlife culture that appeals to both locals and tourists. The majority of the pubs and nightclubs are in Victoria's capital city, although neighboring places such as Beau Vallon and Anse Royale also have alternatives for those looking to party.

Seychelles nightclubs and bars range from informal and laid-back to posh and elegant. Tequila Boom, a Mexican-themed nightclub with live DJs and a dance floor, and Katiolo, a pub with cocktails and a pool table, are two popular venues. Other notable establishments to visit include the Pirate Arms, which has a pirate theme and serves local and imported beers, and La Faya Bar, which has a more upscale atmosphere and a variety of drinks as well as live music.

It's important to keep in mind that the legal drinking age in Seychelles is 18, and bars and nightclubs typically close around 2 or 3 a.m.

Casinos and Gaming

The gaming sector in Seychelles is thriving, with multiple casinos and gaming centers positioned in prominent tourist regions. Many of these casinos have a variety of games to choose from, such as blackjack, poker, roulette, and slot machines. The Gran Kaz in Victoria is the most popular casino on the island, with 100 slot machines and a variety of table games.

Other famous casinos include the Berjaya International Casino in Beau Vallon, which has a VIP lounge and a range of games, and the Club Liberté Casino on the island of Praslin, which has lavish decor and a high-end gaming experience.

It should be noted that gambling is only permitted for visitors in Seychelles, and natives are not permitted to enter the casinos. Visitors must also present their identity and dress correctly to enter the casinos.

Cultural Shows and Events

Cultural exhibits and events are an important aspect of the Seychellois experience since they provide tourists with the opportunity to learn more about the islands' history, traditions, and culture. These events take place throughout the year, with the most popular being the annual Creole Festival in October and the Carnaval International de Victoria in February.

The Creole Festival promotes the country's Creole roots through music, dancing, and gastronomy, whereas the Carnaval International de Victoria is a vibrant celebration that draws performers from all over the world together to demonstrate their talents.

Other cultural events include art exhibitions, theater performances, and traditional artisan fairs, all of which provide insight into Seychelles' rich cultural diversity.

Outdoor Movie Screenings

Outdoor cinema screenings are a one-of-a-kind option to see a movie beneath the stars while visiting Seychelles. Many resorts and hotels host outdoor movie nights for their guests, and public outdoor screenings are held at various locations across the islands. These screenings are typically hosted on the beach or in a park, and they provide a comfortable and laid-back environment in which to sit back, relax, and enjoy a movie with friends or family.

Beau Vallon Beach on Mahé Island, Anse Lazio Beach on Praslin Island, and Anse Source d'Argent on La Digue Island are all popular spots for outdoor movie screenings in Seychelles. The films exhibited during these screenings span from classics to new releases, ensuring that there is something for everyone.

If you want to go to an outdoor movie showing in Seychelles, check the local listings or ask your hotel or resort if there are any forthcoming activities. Bring snacks and drinks, and prepare for a lovely evening beneath the stars.

CHAPTER 7:
SHOPPING IN SEYCHELLES

Shopping in Seychelles provides a one-of-a-kind experience for travelers looking for locally crafted souvenirs, traditional crafts, and luxury items. There is something for everyone in its varied mix of markets, boutiques, and malls. This chapter will look at the best places to shop in Seychelles, including vibrant local markets and posh boutiques.

Seychelles' local markets are a hive of activity where tourists can learn about the country's unique culture and purchase native crafts, spices, and souvenirs. The marketplaces allow you to mingle with people and learn about their daily lives. We will explore the most popular Seychelles local markets, such as the Victoria Market, Beau Vallon Market, and Anse Royale Market.

Seychelles has various retail malls and boutiques for travelers looking for a more upmarket shopping experience. The malls sell foreign brands and luxury things, while the boutiques sell locally manufactured designer apparel, jewelry, and accessories. We will explore the best Seychelles shopping malls and boutiques, such as Eden Plaza, Sir Selwyn Selwyn Clarke Market, and Camion Hall.

This chapter will walk you through the best places to shop in Seychelles, whether you want to bring back a bit of Seychellois culture with traditional crafts or engage in luxury shopping.

Local Markets and Souvenirs

Shopping in Seychelles is an unforgettable experience for both tourists and residents. The local markets are a must-see for anyone wishing to immerse themselves in Seychelles' lively culture. These markets sell a wide variety of locally created goods, including apparel, jewelry, handicrafts, and spices. Visitors can browse the numerous stalls, connect with local sellers, and locate one-of-a-kind treasures to take home with them.

The Sir Selwyn Selwyn Clarke Market, located in Victoria on the island of Mahé, is one of the most prominent markets in Seychelles. This lively market, open every day except Sunday, sells fresh produce, seafood, and spices, as well as homemade crafts and souvenirs. Another popular market in Mahé is the Beau Vallon Market, which sells a variety of local foods and crafts.

Seychelles has various retail malls and stores for visitors seeking a more traditional shopping experience. On Mahé, visitors can explore the Eden Plaza Shopping Center, which features a mix of local and international brands, restaurants, and a cinema. The Anse Royale Shopping Center and the Cable and Wireless Seychelles Complex are two other notable malls.

Whatever type of shopping experience you seek, Seychelles has something for you. Local markets and shopping malls are sure to give you a wonderful experience, whether you're looking for unusual souvenirs or high-end apparel.

Shopping Malls and Boutiques

Aside from local markets and souvenir shops, Seychelles has several shopping malls and boutiques that sell a wide range of high-quality goods. Victoria's capital city is home to various retail malls, including the Eden Plaza and the Sir Selwyn Clarke Market, which have a mix of foreign and local goods.

Eden Plaza is a modern shopping mall with a wide range of shops and eateries, including clothes stores, booksellers, and electronics stores. Visitors can shop for major brands such as Mango and Aldo, as well as local boutiques providing homemade crafts and gifts.

The Sir Selwyn Clarke Market, on the other hand, is a traditional indoor market where locals gather to buy fresh fruit and seafood. However, it also has a section dedicated to souvenirs, where tourists can find goods like woven baskets, coconut shell products, and handmade jewelry.

In addition to shopping malls, the island is home to various high-end stores that sell luxury brands and designer things.

These boutiques can be located in tourist hotspots like Beau Vallon and Anse Royale.

Overall, shopping in Seychelles is diversified, ranging from traditional markets to sophisticated retail malls and high-end boutiques. Unique souvenirs and local products, as well as worldwide brands and luxury items, are available to visitors.

CHAPTER 8:
CULTURE AND FESTIVALS

Seychelles is well-known not just for its spectacular natural beauty and beautiful beaches, but also for its rich cultural past. The Seychellois way of life has been molded by a complex combination of influences from African, Indian, and European cultures. In this chapter, we will look at Seychelles' dynamic culture and festivals, such as its art and music scene, festivals and events calendar, and museums and historical places that provide a peek into the country's past.

Discover Seychelles' lively art and music scene, which is imbued with the country's distinct Creole culture. From traditional Creole music to contemporary performances, the Seychellois music scene provides tourists with a one-of-a-kind and authentic experience. We'll also look at the different music genres that Seychelles is known for and introduce you to some of the country's most skilled musicians.

Seychelles has a full calendar of festivals and events that highlight its culture and traditions throughout the year. From the vibrant Carnaval International de Victoria to the traditional Festival Kreol, these events allow tourists to immerse themselves in Seychelles' distinct culture.

Explore the history and culture of Seychelles at the different museums and historical sites located throughout the islands. The National Museum of History, as well as the plantation buildings and historic ruins, provide an insight into Seychelles' past and the influences that have molded the country's culture.

Whether you enjoy art and music or are interested in history, Seychelles' culture and festivals offer something for everyone. Join me as we take a tour of Seychelles' colorful culture and explore the country's distinct heritage.

Art and Music Scene

Seychelles' art and music scene is a unique representation of the country's eclectic culture and history. The music scene in Seychelles is a combination of several styles, including traditional Creole music, reggae, jazz, and contemporary pop music. Seychelles' traditional Creole music is noted for its vibrant rhythms and appealing beats and is an important component of the country's cultural character.

"Sega," which started with African slaves transported to the islands by French conquerors, is one of the most prominent traditional music traditions in Seychelles. The music is distinguished by a blend of rhythms produced by percussion instruments such as the "rouler" and "katol," as well as the trademark "moutya" dance.

Other historic Seychellois music forms include "kontredanse," a sort of colonial-era ballroom dancing, and "zouk," a popular style of music that originated in the French Caribbean and is recognized for its sensual beats and passionate lyrics.

Seychellois singers have begun to combine contemporary pop and reggae music into their performances in recent years, creating a unique blend of traditional and modern music. The music scene in the country is growing, with frequent concerts and festivals including both local and international performers.

Seychelles' art culture is likewise booming, with a varied spectrum of artistic expressions on show across the country. The Seychelles art scene has something for everyone, from traditional Seychellois handicrafts to modern art displays.

The natural beauty of the islands inspires local artists, who incorporate elements of the breathtaking nature into their creations. Many artists use natural materials to create unique pieces of art that reflect the country's rich culture and history, such as seashells, driftwood, and coconuts.

The Seychelles Art Festival, which takes place annually and brings together local and international artists to present their works, is one of the most important events on the Seychelles art calendar. The festival includes exhibitions, workshops, and performances, and it is an excellent opportunity to get a personal look at the lively Seychellois art scene.

Overall, Seychelles' art and music scenes provide a unique and authentic experience for visitors wishing to learn more about the country's rich cultural legacy. If you enjoy music, art, or are looking for a new cultural experience, Seychelles' vibrant arts scene is not to be missed.

Festivals and Events Calendar

Seychelles is a country that enjoys celebrating its culture, as evidenced by its busy calendar of festivals and events. There is always something going on in Seychelles, from colorful street celebrations to cultural festivals. Here are some of the top festivals and events in Seychelles that you should not miss:

Carnaval International de Victoria - This is one of Seychelles' most popular festivities, drawing thousands of visitors each year. The carnival is a three-day celebration in Victoria's capital city that incorporates colorful floats, live music, and dancing acts. The carnival is a must-see for anybody visiting Seychelles in April and showcases the country's cultural variety.

Festival Kreol - The Festival Kreol is an annual celebration of Creole culture and heritage in the United States. The festival is held in October and includes a number of events such as live music, dancing performances, and traditional Creole cuisine. The event is an excellent opportunity to learn about Seychelles' distinctive culture and meet the friendly natives.

SUBIOS - The Seychelles Festival of the Sea (SUBIOS) is an annual event that honors the country's rich marine heritage. The event includes a variety of activities such as boat races, fishing tournaments, and marine conservation courses. SUBIOS is an excellent approach to learn more about Seychelles' unique marine ecosystem and the significance of its preservation.

Seychelles International Carnival of Victoria - Another popular carnival that takes place in Victoria in April is the Seychelles International Carnival of Victoria. The carnival is a colorful and vibrant celebration that celebrates the cultural diversity of the country. The carnival, which includes live music, dancing performances, and street parties, is a fantastic chance to learn about Seychelles' distinct culture.

Seychelles Arts Festival - The Seychelles Arts Festival honors the country's diverse artistic legacy. The festival includes a variety of art exhibitions, live performances, and seminars and is an excellent chance to immerse yourself in Seychelles' lively art scene.

These are just a few of the numerous festivals and events to look forward to in Seychelles. The country has a bustling and diversified cultural scene, and no matter when you visit, there is always something going on.

Museums and Historical Sites

Seychelles has a number of museums and historical sites that provide insight into the country's history and rich cultural heritage. Here are some of Seychelles' must-see museums and historical sites:

The National Museum of History: Located in Victoria, Seychelles' main city, the National Museum of History provides an in-depth look at the country's natural history, cultural legacy, and colonial history. The museum houses a large collection of items, including traditional Seychellois clothes, tools, and weapons.

The Domaine du Val des Près: This historical monument was formerly the home of Pierre Poivre, a French horticulture who was instrumental in the development of Seychelles' spice trade. The estate has been refurbished and converted into a museum, providing tourists with an insight into Seychelles' colonial past as well as the country's botanical heritage.

The Seychelles Natural History Museum: The Seychelles Natural History Museum, located in Victoria, contains displays that highlight the country's distinctive flora and fauna, such as giant tortoises, rare birds, and marine life. A collection of shells and other marine artifacts is also on display in the museum.

The Bicentennial Monument: The Bicentennial Monument was built in 1978 to commemorate the 200th anniversary of Seychelles' first colonization, and it is a must-see historical site in Victoria. The monument has a bronze statue of a man and woman clutching the Seychellois flag, as well as an inscription that reads "United in happiness and prosperity."

Mission Lodge: Mission Lodge, located on top of a hill in Sans Souci, was once a school for the children of freed slaves. The location has been transformed into a museum, providing visitors with an insight of Seychelles' slave trade and the country's struggle for independence. The museum has exhibits, such as photographs and artifacts, that depict the daily life of the school's pupils.

These museums and historical landmarks provide tourists with a unique opportunity to learn about Seychelles' rich cultural history and colonial past. These sites are a must-see when visiting Seychelles, whether you're a history buff or simply curious about the country's unique flora and fauna.

CHAPTER 9:
7-DAY ITINERARY IN SEYCHELLES

Day 1: Arrival Day

Morning: Arrival and Check-in
Arrive at Mahe International Airport and proceed to your accommodation for check-in. Before embarking on your island trip, take some time to unwind and settle in.

Afternoon: Beau Vallon Beach
Spend the afternoon at Beau Vallon Beach, one of the most popular and colorful beaches in Seychelles. Relax on the smooth sand, swim in the clear seas, and soak up the rays. Snorkeling, jet skiing, and parasailing are among the water sports and activities available at the beach.

Evening: Sunset Cruise
Enjoy a romantic sunset trip in a classic Seychellois sailing boat, where you may gaze out over the shore and the Indian Ocean. While watching the sun set, enjoy some local delicacies and beverages.

Accommodation: Overnight at a hotel or resort on Mahe Island.

If you arrive late in the evening, you may choose to miss the beach and sunset cruise and instead spend the evening relaxing at your resort.

Day 2: Beach Hopping and Water Activities

Morning:

Begin your day with a great breakfast at your lodging. After breakfast, visit one of Seychelles' beautiful beaches. With its dramatic granite boulders and crystal-clear waves, Anse Source D'Argent on La Digue Island is regarded as one of the most beautiful beaches in the world. You can also go to Beau Vallon Beach on Mahé Island, which is great for swimming and water sports.

Afternoon:

Spend the afternoon beach hopping and explore the magnificent coastline of the island. Swim in the invigorating ocean waters at local beaches like Anse Lazio or Anse Intendance. If you're feeling daring, try some water sports like snorkeling, scuba diving, or kayaking. On the island, there are numerous rental firms that provide equipment and guided tours.

Evening:
As the sun sets, return to your lodging to refresh yourself and prepare for dinner. Seychelles boasts a diverse gastronomic scene, including fresh fish and unique Creole delicacies to sample. A romantic supper at one of the island's beachside restaurants or a typical Creole buffet at a local eatery are both options.

Accommodation:
To truly immerse yourself in Seychelles' breathtaking natural beauty, stay at a beachside hotel or guesthouse.

Day 3: Explore the Natural Wonders of Seychelles

Morning:
Visit Praslin Island's Vallée de Mai Nature Reserve, a UNESCO World Heritage site noted for its rare coco de mer palm trees and varied birds. Take a guided tour to learn

more about the reserve's distinctive flora and animals, and then take a lovely walk through the nature trails.

Afternoon:
Take a ferry to La Digue Island and rent a bicycle to explore the island's beautiful beaches, including Anse Source d'Argent, one of the world's most photographed beaches. Swim in the turquoise waves and soak in the stunning environment.

Evening:
Enjoy a seafood meal at one of La Digue's local eateries while watching the sunset over the ocean.

Accommodation:
Return to your Praslin Island lodging or stay overnight on La Digue Island for a more immersive experience.

Day 4: Explore Seychelles' Cultural Side

Morning:
On Mahe Island, visit the George Camille Art Gallery, which features the works of local artists and provides an insight into Seychellois art and culture. The gallery is housed in a lovely colonial-style home surrounded by lush grounds, which adds to the allure of the experience.

Afternoon:
Travel to Victoria, Seychelles' capital city, and tour the Sir Selwyn Selwyn-Clarke Market, a bustling local market where you can buy fresh vegetables, souvenirs, and handicrafts. Spend some time browsing the stalls and chatting with the pleasant vendors.

Evening:
See a traditional Creole dance performance at the Katiolo Cultural Village in Mahe's hills. This cultural center provides a one-of-a-kind and authentic experience where you can learn about Seychelles' history and traditions through music, dance, and storytelling.

Accommodation:

Return to your Mahe Island accommodation or consider staying overnight at Katiolo Cultural Village for a more immersive cultural experience.

Day 5: Cultural and Historical Tour

Morning:

Explore the archipelago's diverse flora and animals at the Seychelles National Botanical Gardens in Victoria, Seychelles' capital city. There are also endemic and exotic palms, fruit bats, huge tortoises, and other species in the gardens.

Afternoon:

Take a guided tour of Victoria and see its historical sites, such as the Victoria Clocktower, which was inspired by London's Little Ben and is a notable icon in the city. Shop for local crafts, souvenirs, and fresh produce at the Sir Selwyn Selwyn-Clarke Market.

Evening:

Enjoy a typical Creole meal with live music and dancing performances at a local restaurant.

Accommodation: Return to your Victoria hotel or explore other parts of Mahé Island.

Day 6: Island Hopping Adventure

Morning:

Take a short flight or ferry to Silhouette, a neighboring island noted for its gorgeous beaches and thick jungles. Take a guided climb through the rainforest to the summit of Mount Dauban, the island's highest peak, for breathtaking views of the surrounding countryside.

Afternoon:

Return to the coast for a snorkeling tour in Silhouette's marine park's crystal-clear waters, where you may see a variety of marine life, including colorful tropical fish, sea turtles, and even reef sharks. Alternatively, enjoy a picnic lunch on one of the island's secluded beaches.

Evening:

Return to your Mahé Island lodgings and dine at one of the island's many seafood restaurants, or sample some native Creole cuisine at a traditional restaurant.

Accommodation:

Spend the night at your Mahé Island lodging.

Day 7: Departure from Seychelles

Morning:

Have one last breakfast at your hotel or resort before taking one more walk on the beach or exploring the nearby area.

Afternoon:

Check out of your hotel and make arrangements for airport transportation. If you have time, you might go last-minute souvenir shopping or visit a neighboring destination.

Evening:

Leave Seychelles with unforgettable memories of its gorgeous islands and welcoming people.

Note: Check your flight schedule ahead of time and plan your departure appropriately to allow for transportation and airport procedures.

CHAPTER 10: PRACTICAL INFORMATION AND TIPS

Customs and Etiquette

When visiting Seychelles, it is critical to understand the country's etiquette and customs in order to have a pleasant and respectful experience. Here are some useful hints and information to remember:

Dress Code: Because Seychelles is a conservative country, it is important to dress modestly when visiting religious places or socializing with people. In public, it is preferable to avoid wearing revealing apparel, shorts, or beachwear. It is acceptable to wear swimsuits to beaches, but make sure to cover yourself when leaving.

Greetings: It is usual to welcome Seychellois people with a handshake, especially when meeting for the first time. As a greeting, you may also hear "bonzour" (good day) or "aloha" (hello) spoken.

Respectful Behavior: Although the people of Seychelles are generally kind and inviting, it is crucial to respect their culture and customs. Avoid using derogatory words or making disparaging remarks, and avoid public demonstrations of affection.

Tipping: Tipping is not customary in Seychelles, but it is appreciated for excellent service at restaurants, cafes, and pubs. Tipping hotel employees, tour guides, and drivers is also usual.

Languages: The official languages of Seychelles are English, French, and Seychellois Creole. Although English is widely spoken, knowing a few basic phrases in French or Creole can be useful when interacting with locals.

Religion: Seychelles is mostly a Christian country, with Catholicism being the dominant religion. When visiting churches, visitors should be respectful of religious sites and traditions, and they should dress modestly.

Transportation: The most frequent means of transportation in Seychelles is by automobile, however, visitors can also explore the islands via bus, taxi, or renting bicycles. Keep in mind that Seychelles follows British road rules, which include driving on the left side of the road.

Currency: The Seychelles rupee (SCR) is the official currency, but major foreign currencies including US dollars and euros, are frequently recognized. Although ATMs and banks are available on the islands, it is best to bring cash for small purchases and transactions.

Visitors can ensure a courteous and delightful trip in Seychelles by keeping these practical recommendations and facts in mind.

Communication and Language

Seychelles' language and communication are greatly affected by the country's varied cultural past. Seychellois Creole, English, and French are the official languages of Seychelles. The most widely spoken language is Seychellois Creole, which is utilized in everyday communication among the natives.

Most Seychellois speak English, which is the language of business, education, and government. French is also widely spoken, especially among the elderly and in the tourism business. English is widely understood and spoken in Seychelles, therefore visitors should have no trouble communicating in it.

Seychellois Creole has a distinct vocabulary and grammar structure that differs from normal French or English. While it may take some time to get used to the local language, most visitors should have no trouble communicating with locals using simple phrases and expressions.

Nonverbal communication is often warm and friendly among Seychellois, and a smile or nod is often enough to indicate warmth and respect. Handshakes are also prevalent, especially in formal situations. It is crucial to note that Seychellois may take offense if they believe they are not being treated with respect, so always be nice and kind.

Visitors to Seychelles should have no trouble conversing with people because English is widely spoken and understood. Learning a few basic phrases in Seychellois Creole can also help to demonstrate respect for the local culture and customs.

Simple Language Phrases to Know

Here are some basic words and phrases you might find useful when visiting Seychelles:

Greeting:

Hello - Bonzour/Bonjou (pronounced "bon-zur/bon-joo")

Goodbye - Orevwar/Bye (pronounced "oh-rev-wahr/bai")

Thank you - Mersi (pronounced "mer-see")

You're welcome - De rien (pronounced "deh ree-en")

Excuse me - Eskiz mwa (pronounced "es-keez mwa")

Sorry - Pardon (pronounced "par-don")

Directions:

Where is...? - Ki kote...? (pronounced "kee koh-teh")

Left - Goche (pronounced "go-sh")

Right - Drwat (pronounced "drah")

Straight ahead - Tou dwit (pronounced "too dweet")

Here - Isi (pronounced "ee-see")

There - La ba (pronounced "lah bah")

Food and Drink:

Menu, please - Menu, silvouple (pronounced "me-noo, seel-voo-play")

Water - Dlo (pronounced "dloh")

Beer - Bier (pronounced "bee-yehr")

Wine - Van (pronounced "vahn")

Coffee - Kafe (pronounced "kah-fay")

Tea - The (pronounced "tay")

Emergency:

Help! - Au secours! (pronounced "oh seh-coor")

I need a doctor - Mwen bezwen yon doktè (pronounced "mwen beh-zwen yohn dok-teh")

Call the police - Rele lapòlis (pronounced "reh-leh la-poh-lees")

I'm lost - Mwen pèdi (pronounced "mwen peh-dee")

Fire! - Larivyè! (pronounced "lah-ree-vee-eh")

These are just a few words to get you started. Learning a few basic phrases in the local language can make your trip more pleasurable and immersive.

Health and Safety Tips

When visiting Seychelles, it is critical to prioritize your health and safety. Here are some pointers to remember:

Vaccinations: Before traveling to Seychelles, make sure you're up to date on regular vaccinations. Furthermore, depending on the length and nature of your trip, you may require additional vaccinations or medications. For recommendations, speak with a healthcare physician or a travel medicine specialist.

Sun protection: Because the Seychelles are close to the equator, the sun can be fierce. To protect your skin and eyes from the sun's harmful rays, wear sunscreen, a hat, and sunglasses.

Water safety: It is critical to use caution and be aware of currents and tides when swimming or participating in water activities. Some beaches may have strong currents, so keep an eye out for any warning signs.

Mosquito-borne illnesses: In the past, Seychelles has seen outbreaks of mosquito-borne illnesses such as dengue fever and chikungunya. Use insect repellent and wear long-sleeved shirts and pants to avoid mosquito bites, especially during peak mosquito hours (dusk and morning).

Food and water safety: Avoid eating or drinking food or water that has not been properly prepared or cooked. It's also a good idea to drink bottled or filtered water to avoid pollution.

Petty crime: Although Seychelles is a safe place, petty crimes such as pickpocketing and stealing sometimes occur. Keep an eye on your valuables and avoid carrying huge sums of cash.

Emergency services: Be aware of the location and contact information for local emergency services, such as hospitals and police. It's also a good idea to get travel insurance in case of any unexpected medical problems.

You may assure a safe and pleasurable journey to Seychelles by following these health and safety precautions

Emergency Contacts

Here are some important contacts to keep in mind in case of an emergency in Seychelles:

Police: 999
Fire Brigade: 999
Ambulance: 151
Seychelles Hospital: +248 4388000

It's also a nice idea to keep your hotel or accommodation's contact details on hand, as well as any emergency contacts provided by your tour operator or travel agency. It is always preferable to be prepared and have critical contacts readily available in the event of an emergency.

Communication and Internet Access

Communication and internet connectivity are widely available in Seychelles, with a variety of choices for remaining connected while on vacation. Here are some ways to stay connected while in Seychelles:

SIM Cards: SIM cards for Seychelles can be acquired at the airport or from a local mobile network provider's store. Cable and Wireless Seychelles (CWS) and Airtel are the two main mobile network providers in Seychelles. Prepaid and postpaid plans for phone, SMS, and data services are available from both carriers.

Wi-Fi: Many hotels, restaurants, and cafes provide their clients with free Wi-Fi. Wi-Fi is also available in most public spaces and at the airport. However, in more remote areas or on smaller islands, the signal may be weaker.

Internet cafés: Most towns in Seychelles have internet cafes where you can pay by the hour for internet access.

Roaming: If you intend to use your phone in Seychelles from your home country, check with your mobile network operator to see if they provide roaming services. Remember that roaming charges can be pricey, so check with your carrier before you go.

It's always a good idea to have various ways to stay connected in case one route fails. Furthermore, it is important to note that internet speeds in Seychelles may be slower than in other countries, particularly in more remote areas.

Useful Apps, Websites, and Maps

Seychelles is a famous tourist destination, and there are numerous applications, websites, and maps available to assist visitors throughout their trip. Here are a few of the most useful:

Seychelles Travel reference App: Available for both Android and iOS devices, this app offers a full reference to Seychelles, including information on attractions, accommodations, restaurants, and more. Offline maps and a currency converter are also included in the program.

Seychelles Travel: This website gives information about Seychelles attractions, lodging, restaurants, and transit alternatives. The website also offers a section with travel recommendations and guest assistance.

Seychelles Interactive Map: This interactive map shows a detailed map of Seychelles and allows users to search for attractions, lodgings, restaurants, and other services. The map also includes a section on Seychelles transit choices.

Google Maps: Google Maps is a popular mapping and navigation program that may be used to locate routes to Seychelles attractions, lodging, and restaurants. The program also features an option for users to download maps for offline use.

XE Currency Converter: This app is a popular currency converter that may be used when traveling in Seychelles to convert currencies. The software is accessible for both Android and iOS devices and contains the most recent currency rates.

WhatsApp: WhatsApp is a popular messaging software that may be used in Seychelles to communicate with locals and fellow visitors. The program can also be used to make Wi-Fi or cellular data-based voice and video conversations.

Facebook and Instagram: Facebook and Instagram are popular social media sites in Seychelles that can be utilized to communicate with locals and fellow tourists. These sites can also be utilized to find information on Seychelles attractions, lodgings, and restaurants.

Travelers may tour Seychelles with ease and make the most of their time in this lovely country by using these apps, websites, and maps.

CONCLUSION

Seychelles is a breathtakingly gorgeous destination with a distinct blend of natural beauties, vibrant culture, and welcoming people. Its magnificent beaches, crystal-clear oceans, and lush landscapes make it a nature lover's paradise, while its rich cultural legacy and festivals provide tourists with a one-of-a-kind and authentic experience.

Seychelles provides something for everyone, whether you want a romantic retreat, a family vacation, or an adventurous excursion. With its year-round warm and sunny weather, it's the ideal spot to visit at any time of year.

While visiting Seychelles, it is critical to respect the local culture and customs, such as dressing modestly, being environmentally conscious, and taking the time to learn a few words in the local language.

Seychelles has an excellent healthcare system and takes visitor safety seriously, so be informed of emergency contacts and take the appropriate precautions to keep safe.

There are numerous options to get around Seychelles, including public transportation, auto rentals, and taxis. It's simple to travel the islands and organize your trip with the use of helpful apps, websites, and maps.

Overall, Seychelles is a once-in-a-lifetime experience that will leave you with lasting memories. Seychelles has it all, whether you want to relax on the beach, discover the natural wonders, or immerse yourself in the colorful culture. So, why delay? Begin organizing your vacation to Seychelles today to witness the magic and beauty for yourself.

Printed in Great Britain
by Amazon